Tiger, T

Story by Beverley Randell
Illustrated by John Boucher

Tiger is asleep.

Mother Monkey is asleep.

Baby Monkey is asleep.

Baby Monkey wakes up.

Here comes Baby Monkey.

Baby Monkey is hungry.

Tiger wakes up.
Tiger is hungry.

Mother Monkey wakes up.

"Baby Monkey!

Come up here!

Come up here!"

Here comes Tiger!

Baby Monkey
is up
in the tree.
Baby Monkey
is **safe**.